PROVERBS

THEOLOGY OF WORK   PROJECT

PROVERBS

THE BIBLE AND YOUR WORK
Study Series

HENDRICKSON
PUBLISHERS

Theology of Work
The Bible and Your Work Study Series: Proverbs

© 2014 by Hendrickson Publishers Marketing, LLC
P.O. Box 3473
Peabody, Massachusetts 01961-3473

ISBN 978-1-61970-524-1

Adapted from the *Theology of Work Bible Commentary*, copyright © 2014
by the Theology of Work Project, Inc. All rights reserved.

William Messenger, Executive Editor, Theology of Work Project
Sean McDonough, Biblical Editor, Theology of Work Project
Patricia Anders, Editorial Director, Hendrickson Publishers

Contributors:
Eileen F. Sommi, "Proverbs" Bible Study
Bruce Waltke and Alice Mathews, "Proverbs and Work" in
the *Theology of Work Bible Commentary*

The Theology of Work Project is an independent, international organization
dedicated to researching, writing, and distributing materials with a biblical
perspective on work. The Project's primary mission is to produce resources
covering every book of the Bible plus major topics in today's workplaces.
Wherever possible, the Project collaborates with other faith-and-work organizations, churches, universities and seminaries to help equip people for
meaningful, productive work of every kind.

Printed in the United States of America

First Printing — November 2014

Contents

The Theology of Work

Work is not only a human calling but also a divine one. "In the beginning God created the heavens and the earth." God worked to create us and created us to work. "The LORD God took the man and put him in the garden of Eden to till it and keep it" (Gen. 2:15). God also created work to be good, even if it's hard to see in a fallen world. To this day, God calls us to work to support ourselves and to serve others (Eph. 4:28).

Work can accomplish many of God's purposes for our lives—the basic necessities of food and shelter, as well as a sense of fulfillment and joy. Our work can create ways to help people thrive. Our work can discover the depths of God's creation. Our work can bring us into wonderful relationships with co-workers and those who benefit from our work (customers, clients, patients, and so forth).

Yet many people face drudgery, boredom, or exploitation at work. We have bad bosses, hostile relationships, and unfriendly work environments. Our work seems useless, unappreciated, faulty, frustrating. We don't get paid enough. We get stuck in dead-end jobs or laid off or fired. We fail. Our skills become obsolete. It's a struggle just to make ends meet. But how can this be if God created work to be good—and what can we do about it? God's answers to these questions must be somewhere in the Bible, but where?

The Theology of Work Project's mission has been to study what the Bible says about work and to develop resources to apply the Christian faith to our work. It turns out that every book of the Bible gives practical, relevant guidance that can help us do our jobs better, improve our relationships at work, support ourselves, serve others more effectively, and find meaning and value in our work. The Bible shows us how to live all of life—including work—in Christ. Only in Jesus can our work be transformed to become the blessing it was always meant to be.

To put it another way, if we are not following Christ during the 100,000 hours of our lives that we spend at work, are we really following Christ? Our lives are more than just one day a week at church. The fact is that God cares about our life *every day of the week*. But how do we become equipped to follow Jesus at work? In the same ways we become equipped for every aspect of life in Christ—listening to sermons, modeling our lives on others' examples, praying for God's guidance, and most of all by studying the Bible and putting it into practice.

This Theology of Work series contains a variety of books to help you apply the Scriptures and Christian faith to your work. This Bible study is one volume in the series The Bible and Your Work. It is intended for those who want to explore what the Bible says about work and how to apply it to their work in positive, practical ways. Although it can be used for individual study, Bible study is especially effective with a group of people committed to practicing what they read in Scripture. In this way, we gain from one another's perspectives and are encouraged to actually *do* what we read in Scripture. Because of the direct focus on work, The Bible and Your Work studies are especially suited for Bible studies *at* work or *with* other people in similar occupations. The following lessons are designed for thirty-minute lunch breaks, although they can be used in other formats as well.

Christians today recognize God's calling to us in and through our work—for ourselves and for those whom we serve. May God use this book to help you follow Christ in every sphere of life and work.

Will Messenger, Executive Editor
Theology of Work Project

Introduction to Proverbs and Work

This study is designed to help you better understand what Proverbs has to say regarding vocation and work. It is by no means exhaustive, but it should give you a strong grasp of what is being offered in this book.

The study will take you on a journey that begins with some basic choices—*the path of righteousness* or *the way of evil, life, or death*. The Valiant Woman from chapter 31 will be our example as we travel down the path of righteousness, learning what is required to become a *wise worker*. Along the road, wisdom and understanding will cry out the way to go, reminding us that we are not alone. We will be undergirded with the fear and awe of the Lord, becoming more aware each day that we can only walk this path of righteousness in humility before God. It is a lifelong journey. Temptations will come. Mistakes will be made. But in the end, if we walk in awe of God, listening to wisdom and receiving instruction, God's promise of life and goodness is ours.

It is worth considering your approach when beginning this study. While Proverbs does present itself as an aid to those who want to become better persons or achieve prosperity and success, it holds fast to the truth that wisdom can only truly grow in relationship to God. If you are striving to become a better, more successful person, Proverbs will be helpful. But the pearl of Proverbs lies in becoming a person of wisdom who reflects God's very character—which is impossible to attain without knowing God.

Within each chapter in this study are three lessons that will explore the book of Proverbs and how it instructs us in regard to work. Biblical references are noted at the start of the lessons that you should read before you get started. In each lesson you will also find "Food for Thought" sections with discussion questions based on the current lesson. Feel free to use them or come up with your own questions to spur your group to engage with the text and topic at hand. The questions will also help your group members get to know one another better as the lessons progress. There is also a "Closing Prayer" at the end of each lesson to use if you want. Use your discretion and follow God's prompting as you pray. Even though there is no prayer prompt at the start of each lesson, consider opening each lesson with prayer to help focus your attention and prepare you for all that is available as you read, study, converse, and pray with your group. Enjoy your time in God's word. May it draw you closer to the One who loves you beyond measure.

Chapter 1

Preparing for the Road Ahead

Before taking a trip, we usually prepare ourselves. We learn in advance about the place we are visiting. We decide what to bring and what to leave behind. We check our directions and coordinate where and when to meet others along the way. So it is as we begin Proverbs. The lessons in this chapter will introduce us to the book of Proverbs and prepare us for the way ahead.

Lesson #1: A Road Map for Success (Proverbs 1:1–6)

Introduction to Proverbs

How often have you complained, "I wish someone had told me that when I started this job"? The pitfalls that could have been avoided if you only had known better. Proverbs is a book of sayings, advice, instructions, warnings, and examples to help guide you on the path you have chosen, an instruction manual for life and work.

Throughout the ancient Near East, rulers commissioned numerous sages to collect the accepted wisdom of their nations for the instruction of their young people entering into various professions. In Proverbs, we see King Solomon as the chief author of a wisdom manual for people of all ages. The proverbs challenge us to seek wisdom from the Lord ourselves.

In 2 Chronicles 1:1–13 we learn that Solomon, the son of King David, was ruling securely over the nation of Israel. One night

Solomon went up to the tabernacle to worship and offer sacrifices to the Lord. During that night the Lord appeared to Solomon and asked him what he wanted as king. Solomon asked for "wisdom and knowledge" so he could rule God's people.

God was pleased that Solomon asked for wisdom and knowledge rather than the predictable requests of long life, riches, honor, and success. So God not only made Solomon the wisest man who ever lived, but also the wealthiest man of his time (1 Kgs. 3:12). It is this wisdom that King Solomon put into the proverbs, and we continue to be the fortunate recipients of its content.

 Food for Thought

Take a minute and remember some of the sound advice you received through the years from those you respected. Share these "pearls of wisdom" with the group. If God appeared to you tonight as he did to King Solomon and asked you what you wanted, how would you respond?

_____

_____

_____

_____

_____

Studying Proverbs

There are some books you can read and digest in a sitting. Proverbs isn't one of them. Studying Proverbs is a lifelong endeavor, one that requires using its sayings and teachings as touchstones as we slowly develop virtue, character, and an awe of God. The book is divided into seven collections addressing a variety of character issues, behaviors, scenarios, and truths, as well as offering practical advice. There are anecdotes, lessons in contrast, repetition, and a call to fear the Lord. The proverbs tell us that good work habits generally lead to prosperity and flow out of good character formed by an awe of God. There are more proverbs about wise speech than any other topic, and issues of work and money run a close second.

This study will work through the book of Proverbs topically, circling around to various teachings instead of following a linear pattern. We will stand together at the start of this journey with choices to make, an example to follow, and a call to heed. We will study qualities and characteristics of the wise worker, such as trustworthiness, diligence, shrewdness, generosity, justice, sound speech, and modesty. All the while, wisdom will shout to us in the street and understanding will lift up her voice on top of the heights beside the way (Prov. 1:20; 8:1). They will implore us to listen, to take their instruction so that things might go well for us.

 Food for Thought

If you have studied Proverbs before, is there any proverb in particular that you remember? Open the book, find a proverb you like, and share it with the group. What do you anticipate the most as you begin to study Proverbs? What do you hope to gain?

Closing Prayer

Give God thanks for his inspired word. Pray for each person in the group, giving thanks for colleagues who stand in awe of God and who desire to grow in wisdom and understanding.

Lesson #2: A Shining Example (Proverbs 31:10–31)

The Valiant Woman

If we want to get better at our work—whether we want to be a better manager, employee, parent, or shopkeeper—it helps to have a good example. At the very end of Proverbs is the supreme example of the wise worker and partner. Various translations of the Bible have used different words to describe her, such as "excellent," "noble," "virtuous," and "capable." The original Hebrew word used to identify her is *chayil*, meaning "strength," as in the strength of a warrior. Since the word *valiant* captures both the strength and virtue of this woman, we will refer to her as the Valiant Woman throughout our study.

The Valiant Woman is the wise manager of diverse enterprises, ranging from weaving to winemaking to trade in the market. She finds fulfillment in her work, and its success makes her husband "known in the city gates" (31:23). This woman is full of strength and virtue, working as an entrepreneur with a household enterprise along with servants/workers to manage. You cannot help but be impressed as the text extols her diligence, ability, trustworthiness, value, strength, dignity, discernment, and preparedness. She is amazing and a great example for us to follow.

As we study the many characteristics of a wise worker, it will help to keep the Valiant Woman's example in the forefront as we imagine these qualities at play in the workplace. To picture the Valiant Woman considering a field to purchase and using her earnings to plant a vineyard, while diligently working to ensure her household is well taken care of and the needs of the poor are met, can do nothing but inspire us.

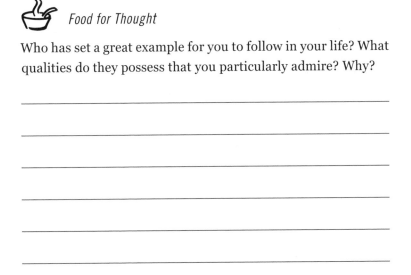 *Food for Thought*

Who has set a great example for you to follow in your life? What qualities do they possess that you particularly admire? Why?

_____

_____

_____

_____

_____

_____

What Is the Source of Her Wisdom and Success?

It's easy for us to read Proverbs 31 and notice the Valiant Woman's work ethic and virtues. She is tireless as she rises before dawn to feed her family and staff. She does not "eat the bread of idleness" (31:27) and is busy planting vineyards, buying fields, weaving linens, and managing her household. The Valiant Woman delights in her work. She finds satisfaction and joy in it as she sees it produce good things, enabling her to provide for her family and the many people under her care. The Valiant Woman has time to help the needy, teach kindness to others, engage in conversation, and be good to her husband. Her work isn't all-consuming. In the midst of her work responsibilities, she has the flexibility and willingness to stop, lend a hand, and invest in others.

At the end of Proverbs 31, after all the Valiant Woman's abilities and virtues are described and extolled, the source of her wisdom is revealed: "A woman who fears the LORD is to be praised" (31:30). The Valiant Woman is someone who chose the path of righteousness and lived in fear of the Lord. This produced in her wisdom to live a humble, productive, and profitable life that brought glory to God, praise from man, and help to those around her.

 Food for Thought

How does the way of wisdom flow out of the fear of the Lord? Use personal examples in your discussion.

_____

_____

_____

_____

_____

_____

_____

_____

Closing Prayer

Thank God for the good example of the Valiant Woman. Ask the Lord to teach you what it means to live in fear of him.

Lesson #3: Fear of the Lord (Proverbs 1:7; 3:8; 8:13; 9:10; 10:27; 14:26–27; 15:33; 19:23; 22:4; 31:30)

First Things First!

Have you ever had a teacher, manager, parent, or leader of some sort use the phrase, "First things first!"? A group is gathered, about to start a project or embark on a new endeavor, and as the leader is about to give instructions and fill in some details, the group hears, "But before we start, first things first!" Well, that is where we are.

This first chapter's purpose is to prepare us for the road ahead. The first lesson was meant to give us a general understanding of what the book of Proverbs is about. The second lesson cast a vision for what a person is like who truly lives in awe of God and walks in wisdom and understanding. But with the introduction and the vision of the Valiant Woman cast, we cannot really begin until we understand what it means to fear the Lord.

 Food for Thought

Looking back on Lessons #1 and #2, what are your thoughts about the book of Proverbs and the example of the Valiant Woman? Before we look at what it means to fear the Lord, what do you think it means?

_____

_____

_____

_____

_____

"The Fear of the Lᴏʀᴅ"

This phrase could possibly be one of the most misunderstood phrases in the Bible. As usual, when reading the Bible we must take things in context. In 2 Timothy 1:7, Paul writes how God did not gives us a "spirit of cowardice." In this context, he is talking about a timid, fearful spirit. In Proverbs, the fear of the Lord is "an attitude of respect toward God, which includes a healthy dread of displeasing him" (William E. Berkley, *Expository Files* 4.9 [September 1997]). Merriam-Webster's dictionary defines *fear* as "profound reverence and awe especially toward God." Understanding this concept is crucial since it is the foundation of the entire book of Proverbs. Without the fear of the Lord, we will never be able to walk the path of righteousness. Since walking the path of righteousness requires wisdom and understanding, and since wisdom and understanding are born from the fear of the Lord, we must understand this attitude of the heart and allow it to take root in our lives.

Adopting an attitude of fear concerning the Lord keeps us from caving in to our own sinful nature. How many of us can remember the trouble we avoided in childhood due to a healthy fear of our parents? If we do not fear the Lord, bad things will happen. The Lord wants us to fear him because his desires for us are good. He knows that a healthy fear of the Lord will cause good things to happen as we abide in the safety of his love, commandments, and parameters. The following verses note what a fear of the Lord produces or causes. Read them together: Proverbs 1:7; 3:7; 8:13; 10:27; 14:26; 15:16; 23:17; and 24:21.

 Food for Thought

After reading the references listed at the start of this lesson and the ones above, discuss the benefits of fearing the Lord God Almighty. How is having a healthy fear of the Lord different from being afraid of God? If you can view the online video "Awe of God Informs the Heart" (in the section "What Do the Proverbs Have to Do with Work?" in "Proverbs and Work," at www.theologyofwork.org), discuss how Ken Duncan, one of the most important photographers of our time, lives in awe of God and how his work reflects this posture of living in "fear of the LORD."

_____

_____

_____

_____

_____

_____

_____

_____

Closing Prayer

Ask the Lord to forgive you for not always living in awe and fear of him. Pray that your understanding of what it means to fear the Lord will deepen throughout this study. Thank God for all the blessings that this attitude of the heart produces.

Chapter 2

The Wise Worker Is Trustworthy

Along the path of righteousness, there are behaviors the Lord asks us to practice. Our behavior is always a reflection of who we are and whom we ultimately serve. Our actions should reflect God's character, and our lives should emulate the life of Christ by the grace and power of the Holy Spirit.

Lesson #1: Does Your Work Benefit Those Around You? (Proverbs 3:7; 10:18; 18:9; 29:24; 31:10–31)

Those above You

Can you remember the first time an adult looked you in the eyes when you were still a child and asked, "Can I count on you?" Maybe a parent was asking you to watch over a sibling in their absence. Maybe a coach was asking you to step up in leadership for the team. Perhaps a store manager was leaving you alone in the shop for a while. As you stepped into the situation, no doubt feelings of honor, fear, excitement, and hope stirred in you. If you felt ready and prepared for the moment, you wanted nothing more than to prove yourself trustworthy.

One of the first things mentioned about the Valiant Woman in Proverbs 31:10–31 is that the heart of her husband trusted her. What a gift. Are you that person? Are you the person that your supervisor, CEO, or president can trust to do the right thing? Are you someone to whom others turn in order to get the job done right? When the going gets tough and the need is great, does your phone ring? A wise worker is someone who is faithful to the mission and all those working toward the mission. If you are to be considered a trustworthy person, your work must bring good to those who hired you.

We have all been in work situations that were less than ideal. No matter what the situation, wise workers adhere to their ethical duty to do good despite the bad. Proverbs teaches that we must not steal from our employer (29:24), vandalize (18:9), or slander in order to air our grievances (10:18). We owe our employers our faithful and right behavior no matter what. We are people of God, and difficult circumstances do not change who we are and how we behave. No matter how hard it is to rise above a tough situation, God is glorified and your virtue is intact when your behavior remains righteous.

 Food for Thought

Do you remember an early time in your life when, because of what someone saw in you, you were asked to take on more responsibility? What qualities do you think that person saw in you? How do we rise above difficult situations and walk in righteousness as faithful, trustworthy, wise workers?

Those under Your Care

There is nothing better and more secure than being under the care of someone who always has your best interest and welfare in mind. When you can live without looking over your shoulder because there is a trustworthy person in charge of your situation, it is a blessing that enables you to spend your time being productive instead of worrying.

Isn't that what we have in God, who loves us, knows our needs, and cares about our futures? God is faithful and we can trust him in every way. Solomon's father, King David, was effusive about God's faithfulness throughout the book of Psalms. The following references from David and other psalmists testify to God's faithfulness: Psalm 36:5–6; 89:1–2, 8, 14; 91:4; and 117:1–2.

Under God's care, we have great refuge and peace. As Christ-followers, shouldn't those under our care share the same benefit? Again, the Valiant Woman is our model. Her work benefits her customers (Prov. 31:14), her community (Prov. 31:20), her immediate family (Prov. 31:12, 28), and her co-workers (Prov. 31:15). She "looks well to the ways of her household" (Prov. 31:27), and those who work for her trust her, those who depend on her "rise up and call her happy" (Prov. 31:28). She is someone everyone can count on to do good. Can those under your care count on you?

 ### Food for Thought

Do you live in peace knowing that God is trustworthy and faithful? Do you think that those above you and under your care consider you to be a trustworthy person? If so, why? If not, why not?

_____

_____

_____

_____

_____

_____

Closing Prayer

Thank God for his faithfulness. Ask him to help you grow as a person who can be trusted. Ask forgiveness for anything that demands repentance. "If we confess our sins, he who is faithful and just will forgive us our sins and cleanse us from all unrighteousness" (1 John 1:9).

Lesson #2: Honest Words (Prov. 6:16–19; 10:18; 12:22; 14:25; 19:5)

Truth-Tellers

We are the people of God, so we're supposed to be different. Wouldn't it be great if a synonym for "Christian" in our culture was "truth-teller"? The proverbs constantly encourage us to serve the Lord by telling the truth to the people around us.

> Lying lips are an abomination to the LORD, but those who act faithfully are his delight. (Prov. 12:22)

> Truthful lips endure forever, but a lying tongue lasts only a moment. (Prov. 12:19)

> I will speak noble things, and from my lips will come what is right; for my mouth will utter truth; wickedness is an abomination to my lips. (Prov. 8:6–7)

The rest of the Bible concurs that telling the truth is highly valued by God. Honesty is addressed in the Mosaic Law (Lev. 19:11), the Ten Commandments (Exod. 20:16), and the new life of the believer (Col. 3:9). It is a virtue "grounded ultimately in the character of

God—that is, we are to be truthful because God is truthful" (see "Truthtelling is the Norm in the Bible," in "Truth and Deception Overview" at www.theologyofwork.org).

If we commit ourselves to honesty at all times no matter the cost, embarrassment, inconvenience, or difficulty, it's amazing how much trouble we can avoid and how much clarity we can gain. When we are not committed to honesty, little white lies sneak into our speech, one lie leads to another, and suddenly our waters are muddy and our relationships compromised. An "innocent lie" ends up hurting someone. People make decisions based on your lie, and then what was supposed to happen never does. We forget what we lied about and can't keep up with the trail of dishonesty that ultimately results in some embarrassing situations and, most damaging, a lack of credibility. Lying makes a mess of things and never pays the dividends we expect. Heeding God's call to speak the truth in all circumstances will certainly develop your reputation as a trustworthy worker.

 Food for Thought

When are you tempted to lie? How common and acceptable is lying in your workplace? Why is it that way? Do the lies told in your workplace actually work? What steps of action or accountability measures can you take to help you remain honest in your speech/communication?

_____

_____

_____

_____

_____

An Abomination to God

Your reputation as a trustworthy person, however, shouldn't be the only thing keeping you from dishonesty. Lying lips are said to conceal hatred, and the one who slanders is considered a fool (Prov. 10:18). Proverbs reveals that lying is an "abomination to the LORD" (12:22). Proverbs 6:16–19 talks about seven things God finds detestable. Two of them have to do with dishonesty—a lying tongue and a false witness who utters lies. God hates lying. His word calls it an abomination and one who utters lies is named a betrayer. According to Proverbs, liars will not go unpunished nor will they escape.

As Christians, we are a reflection of Christ—who is "the way, the *truth*, and the life" (John 14:6; emphasis added). As a result, we should resemble the One we serve by living truth-filled lives. It is part of our testimony as believers. As always, God's admonitions for us are for our good. Lying brings with it all kinds of trouble, heartache, negative consequences, and ultimately death. But truth always leads to life and freedom (John 8:32).

 Food for Thought

How does knowing that God finds lying detestable affect you? Share with the group an example of a truthful person and how their example inspires you. How does truth bring freedom?

_____

_____

_____

_____

_____

Closing Prayer

Ask the Lord to make you sensitive to any and all falsehood in your speech. Ask God to forgive you for the lies you have told. Pray for strength, determination, awareness, and obedience as you choose truth each day at work.

Lesson #3: Honest Deeds (Proverbs 11:1–3; 13:5; 15:2; 16:11; 20:14, 17, 23; 23:10–11)

Are You a Person of Integrity?

God calls us not only to honesty in word but also to honesty in deed. "The wicked *act* shamefully and disgracefully" (Prov. 13:5; emphasis added). To the believer, James says that faith, unless accompanied by action, is dead (2:17). The world should not only *hear* the truth from Christians, it should also *see* it in our lives. Our honesty should be on display in our financial statements, contracts, marketing campaigns, sales tactics, and advertisements, how we respond to the cashier who has given us too much change, and what we do in the stockroom when no one is watching. People of integrity are those known for "meaning what they say and saying what they mean." They are not only right-speaking but also right-acting. In 2 Timothy 3:16–17, Paul teaches us that the inspired word of God is profitable for teaching and training us in righteousness so that "everyone who belongs to God may be proficient, equipped for every good work."

In Proverbs 20:23, the use of false weights and measures describes the act of defrauding a customer. Proverbs 23:10–11 addresses land ownership, forbidding the moving of landmarks to increase one's own property. These examples establish the principle that dishonest acts are as abhorrent to the Lord as dishonest words.

 *Food for Thought*

How do you hold yourself accountable for right actions at work? How do you avoid the temptation to act dishonestly? Are there any "gray areas" in your workplace that cloud your judgment when making honest choices?

_____

_____

_____

_____

_____

_____

_____

_____

An Opportunity to Delight the Lord

Honest business practices are a delight to the Lord (Prov. 11:1). Since this is so, we should be inspired to bless him by the integrity we practice in the workplace. In a 2013 speech at Kiros Seattle, Brian Isaac Bauer said, "God is passionate about honesty in business. . . . Making a deal that's accurate, fair, and honest is something that pleases God. We as business men and women should be encouraged that God is delighted when we do our job with integrity" (see "God Loves Honest Scales in Finance," in "Proverbs and Work" at www.theologyofwork.org).

We have a high calling in life to be people of integrity—honest in word and deed. With the inspired word of God that trains us in righteousness, the accountability found in Christian fellowship, and the work of the Holy Spirit, we can be people of integrity who delight the Lord and who bring glory to his name as workers who can be trusted in word and deed.

 Food for Thought

How does living in a healthy fear of the Lord help you remain honest in your work? Share an example of someone in your life who is a person of great integrity. What have they taught you? Since honesty is an aspect of trustworthiness—a goal of the wise worker—the next question is whether people can trust what you say and do. How do you answer that question?

_____

_____

_____

_____

_____

_____

_____

_____

Closing Prayer

Thank God for his word and for the clarity the Bible brings regarding how we are supposed to live in a world that is full of compromise. Meditate on the fact that the Lord delights in good business practice. Pray for one another.

Chapter 3

The Wise Worker Is Diligent

"It is when we stop doing our best work that our enthusiasm for the job wanes. We must motivate ourselves to do our very best, and by our example lead others to do their best as well."
—S. Truett Cathy, founder/owner Chick-fil-A

Lesson #1: The Virtue of Hard Work (Proverbs 10:4–5, 26; 12:11, 27; 21:5; 24:30–34; 31:13, 15, 16, 24)

Willing Hands

The woman in Proverbs 31 is certainly a model of diligence. She plants vineyards, makes linen garments and sells them, rises before dawn to start providing for her household, gathers food from afar, shops for wool and flax, strengthens herself, and works to help those who are less fortunate. Talk about hardworking! Proverbs 31:13 says that she works with "willing hands," meaning that all this hard work is *her*. She is not a frazzled, overworked manager carrying out her long list of duties with a heavy sigh. She is a willing, content worker using her skills wisely and making a great contribution.

The Valiant Woman makes things happen and affords opportunities to those around her. Her diligence provides jobs for many others, products for the community at large, and income for her family to live well. Her household is not a burden to society but makes a contribution. In this example the fruit of her diligence is good and plenty.

 *Food for Thought*

Proverbs 31:13 notes that the Valiant Woman works with "willing hands." What does this mean to you and how can you apply the concept to your work?

_____

_____

_____

_____

_____

_____

_____

_____

A Shining Example

Dale Crownover, the president of Texas Nameplate, is a firm believer in hard work. He attributes the success of his company to 2 Chronicles 15:7, which says, "But you, take courage! Do not let your hands be weak, for your work shall be rewarded" (see the video "Faith, Work and Quality" online at "Proverbs and Work," www.theologyofwork.org). Having taken over the family business when bankruptcy threatened years ago, he not only turned the company around but elevated it to a place of national prominence. In 1998, when Texas Nameplate—with about fifty employees, most of whom didn't even have a high school degree—won the Malcolm Baldrige National Quality Award, they were the smallest company ever to win.

Dale Crownover believes the Bible teaches that if you work hard, you will be rewarded. Ever the pragmatist, he likes to challenge people by saying that "at some point you have to quit praying and go to work. I'm all for praying, but God wants you to go out and get to work doing all this." Practical advice from a diligent man.

 Food for Thought

Would you consider yourself a hardworking person? Explain. How can you grow in this area? How does hard work glorify God? Is there anyone in your life who taught you the value of hard work?

_____

_____

_____

_____

_____

_____

_____

_____

Closing Prayer

Thank God for good examples—for the people who inspire us. Ask your group members how you can pray for them at work, and spend some time praying for one another and your jobs.

Lesson #2: The Good Sense of Planning Ahead
(Proverbs 6:6–11; 10:4; 13:4; 16:1; 19:15, 21; 20:4;
21:5, 25; 24:27; 26:14–15; 27:1, 23–27; 28:2; 31:14, 16)

The Valiant Woman and the Ant

Diligence isn't just about hard work; it also involves planning ahead. The Valiant Woman plans ahead. "She brings her food from far away" (Prov. 31:14), meaning that she doesn't depend on last-minute convenience purchases of questionable quality and cost. She "considers a field" (Prov. 31:16) before buying it, investigating its long-term potential as a vineyard that will take at least two or three years of tending before it produces its first crop. The point is that she makes decisions based on their long-term consequences. Proverbs 21:5 tells us that "the plans of the diligent lead surely to abundance, but everyone who is hasty comes only to want."

Proverbs 6:6–11 advises us to look at an ant's life. As a kid, did you ever watch ants work as they marched in and out of their ant-hills carrying food? They are fascinating and tireless. Research shows that ants can pull objects fifty times their body weight. "They are abundant, diverse, and possess surprising ingenuity" (F. J. Viljoen, "Ants: Creatures with 'Character'"). As Proverbs urges us to look at the ant and its ways, what can we learn from this creature?

For one thing, ants tend to be hardworking. No one has to tell them to get going! Ants also plan for the future. Proverbs 6:8 says the ant "prepares its food in the summer, and gathers its sustenance in harvest." Planning ahead takes many forms in workplaces. Financial planning is mentioned in Proverbs 24:27: "Prepare your work outside, get everything ready for you in the field; and after that build your house." In other words, don't start building your house until your fields are producing the necessary funds to finish your construction project. Jesus picked up on this in Luke 14:28–30: "Which of you, intending to build a tower, does not first sit down and estimate the cost, to see whether he has enough to complete it? Otherwise, when he has laid a foundation and is not able to finish, all who see it will begin to ridicule him, saying, 'This fellow began to build and was not able to finish.'" Although Proverbs is not a planning manual for modern business, it reminds us that long-term planning is a godly pursuit.

 Food for Thought

What is your "take-away" from the examples of the Valiant Woman and the ant? What long-term plans do you have, and how are you investing in making them come true? What exactly could you do in your work today that will put you in a better position next year, five years from now, ten years from now? Are there sacrifices you need to make today in order to fulfill God's plans for you in the future?

_____

_____

_____

_____

_____

_____

_____

Laugh at the Future

Sprinkled throughout Proverbs are admonitions to plan for the future—whether it be in the example of the cycle of agricultural asset management (27:23–27), the ruler who thinks long term (28:2), or building a house (24:27). There is wisdom in planning ahead that yields peace. In Proverbs 31:21, we see that the Valiant Woman is not afraid of the winter because she knows her household is prepared with proper clothing. In verse 25, she "laughs at the time to come," knowing she is prepared for what lies ahead.

God knows we are better able to live in peace if we work hard and plan for our futures. His instruction is always for our good. Unlike God, however, we cannot control what happens to our plans and therefore we need to remind ourselves of Proverbs 27:1, which instructs us to "not boast about tomorrow, for you do not know what a day may bring." But in faith, we plan with wisdom, speak with humility, and live in expectation that God's plans are our ultimate desire.

 Food for Thought

Discuss the positive results you've experienced by planning ahead and the consequences you've suffered from not planning ahead. Think about ways in which God plans ahead, and discuss.

_____

_____

_____

_____

_____

Closing Prayer

Think about what you just studied. Is there anything in it that speaks directly to you? Ask God to give you strength, endurance, and the will to do all he has called you to. What are you in need of today? Ask it in Jesus' name.

Lesson #3: Add Value (Proverbs 18:9; 21:5; 22:29; 31:10, 13, 18, 24)

What Do You Add to the Job?

Have you ever heard someone at work say, "I'm just putting in my time"? This worker may not be a sluggard, but they are certainly not an example of a wise worker. Proverbs teaches us not just to be hardworking and busy, but also to be people who add value to the workplace.

It is obvious that the Valiant Woman is not only hardworking but is also someone who adds great value overall. In Proverbs 31:18, she "perceives that her merchandise is profitable," and the products she sells bring her praise in the gates of the city. Proverbs 31:26 says that she also speaks wisdom and teaches kindness. When you look at the Valiant Woman's accomplishments, the response of her children and husband, and the fact that she "looks well to the ways of her household" (31:27), the value added by her work, presence, personality, and virtues is great. The Valiant Woman doesn't only work hard and long; she also works smart, adding value to the household and creating high-quality products.

 *Food for Thought*

How do you add value to your work and your workplace? How does this particular aspect of diligence energize you? How can you increase your value as a worker?

_____

_____

_____

_____

_____

_____

_____

The Importance of Profit

It is important to keep in mind that these proverbs are grounded in God's character. Proverbs 18:6 compares a lazy worker to a vandal, and Proverbs 21:5 extols the diligent worker whose plans lead to abundance. God wants us to work profitably. It isn't enough to simply complete our assigned tasks and punch a clock. We must care about whether or not our work adds value to the materials, capital, and labor consumed. We perform a godly service when we make it possible for businesses to operate profitably. Even if working for a nonprofit organization, all workers should pay attention to how their work furthers the mission of the organization.

How could the Valiant Woman buy a field, provide for her household, support those in need, extend a hand to the poor, and laugh at the days to come if she wasn't operating from an overflow?

Christians sometimes view profit with suspicion, and its reputation has been sullied by companies that put profit ahead of human flourishing. Making a profit must always be done in righteousness—not by cheating buyers, employees, suppliers, lenders or shareholders. Wise workers reflect the character of God when they work hard and smart, producing a profit and adding value to the work, organization, or mission.

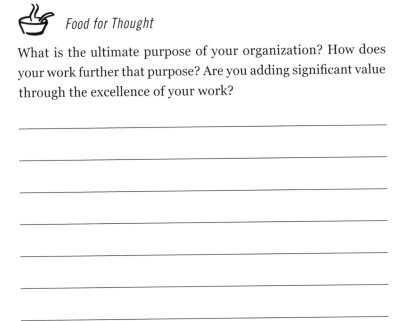 *Food for Thought*

What is the ultimate purpose of your organization? How does your work further that purpose? Are you adding significant value through the excellence of your work?

_____

_____

_____

_____

_____

_____

_____

_____

Closing Prayer

Ask the Lord to bless your work and your company, organization, or mission. Ask God to show you how to add value and profitability to your work. Thank him for the opportunity of the work before you.

Chapter 4

The Wise Worker Is Shrewd

The Valiant Woman sets an example of exceptional acumen in her work. The book of Proverbs describes this virtue as being "prudent" (Prov. 19:14) or "shrewd" (Prov. 1:4). We may tend to think of shrewd people as those who take advantage of others, but in Proverbs the word *shrewdness* carries the idea of making the most of resources and circumstances. If we understand shrewdness as "clever, discerning awareness and hardheaded acumen," then we see the kind of shrewd wisdom God intends for workers.

Lesson #1: Alert and Prepared (Proverbs 1:4; 8:12, 15–16; 19:14; 22:3; 31:13–14, 21–23)

On Your Toes

Walking the path of righteousness requires attentiveness, purpose, and determination. You cannot just stroll along and believe things are going to go well for you. You must be aware of the opportunities and challenges along the way, as well as the stumbling blocks and distractions. Being "on your toes" means being alert and ready for anything. Wise workers don't only have their eyes focused on their work, but they are also aware of what is happening around them. If you are shrewd, you are conscious of shifts in the market, consumer satisfaction, new products, political change, organizational restructuring, your competition, destructive ploys, and available opportunities. You analyze how you can capitalize on opportunities and developments and help your organization adjust and adapt. A shrewd person is never oblivious.

God wants his people to have a discerning awareness. Romans 12:2 says, "Do not be conformed to this world, but be transformed by the renewing of your minds, so that you may discern what is the will of God—what is good and acceptable and perfect." At our work and throughout life, there will be decisions to make where judgment must be exercised. Our shrewdness will play a critical role. Whether you are hiring a new employee, adopting a new organizational model, signing a contract with an investor, leaving your job, changing careers, or dealing with personnel, the more insightful and prudent you are, the more successful you will be in any given situation.

Proverbs 8 tells us that wisdom and prudence live together, that they operate hand in hand. We see the Valiant Woman's shrewdness displayed as she sources her materials of wool and flax. She doesn't just use what is right in front of her, she seeks out the right materials. We see her gathering her food from different places, no doubt getting the best quality at the best price, along with variety. "She is like the ships of the merchant, she brings her food from far away" (31:14). In verses 16 and 18, we see her "considering a field" before she buys it and perceiving that "her merchandise is profitable." Our Valiant Woman is shrewd in her business dealings, using her wisdom and prudence to care for her family and enterprises—just as we are called to do.

 Food for Thought

Are you naturally a person who makes it your business to know what is going on around you? How has being aware of your environment and the people in it been beneficial in your work? When has acting shrewdly served you well? Have you ever thought of shrewdness as a negative characteristic? If so, can you see how it is a godly one?

_____

_____

_____

_____

_____

_____

_____

Locked and Loaded

In the military, "locked and loaded" is slang for "weapons loaded and prepared for firing." Outside of a military situation, it simply means you are ready to go, prepared on all fronts. Being shrewd involves a level of preparedness that goes beyond the immediate.

Have you ever known a mother who was always prepared for whatever situation might arise? When she left home, her bag contained a variety of items for "just in case." There was food in case someone got hungry and extra clothing in case someone got wet or dirty. There were extra toys and books in case someone got bored and, of course, there was the blanket, pacifier, and bottle, just in case someone needed comfort, sleep, or a drink. She was prepared for just about anything. She was a shrewd parent.

The same holds true in other kinds of work. If you are a wise worker, you prepare for the unexpected. You have a contingency plan. Special-events planners know what they will do if too few or too many people show up. They are ready with a backup plan if the sound system crashes. They know where they will go if the weather doesn't hold. Similarly, shrewd trial attorneys show up to court with a thorough understanding of their adversary's strategy. They are prepared for whatever the adversary may throw at them. They know the answer to every question before it is asked. They anticipate the adversary's arguments and have a rebuttal ready. They know what the witnesses will say before they say it, and they are prepared with evidence to impeach the witness who tries to stretch the truth.

In Proverbs 31:21–22, we see the Valiant Woman in all her wisdom prepared for the days ahead. She is not afraid of the snow, "for all her household are clothed in crimson. She makes herself coverings; her clothing is fine linen and purple." Being prepared for the moment and what could possibly come your way is one of the marks of the wise worker.

 Food for Thought

Are you typically prepared like the mother, special-events planner, or trial attorney mentioned? How can you increase your level of preparedness so that you are even better equipped for the work at hand? When have you not been as prepared as you could have been and what were the consequences? Discuss how your preparation has blessed you and those around you.

Closing Prayer

Ask the Lord for wisdom and an increased ability to be aware, prepared, insightful, and resourceful. Thank him for your job and ask him to bless your work.

Lesson #2: Help and Counsel (Proverbs 10:17; 11:14; 13:20; 15:22; 19:23; 20:18; 21:30; 27:17)

No Shame in Asking

As Jim Collins noted in his book *Good to Great*, the most effective leaders of the best companies display a paradoxical blend of personal humility and professional will. They are people willing to listen to others' opinions and advice, ask questions, and admit mistakes. They are ready to promote and empower people around them and lead by example in a spirit of service. They know that the best outcomes, products, campaigns, designs, logistics, and processes are birthed from a collaborative effort that considers multiple points of view. Sometimes the word *humble* can elicit images of a person who is timid, insecure, and weak. But in reality, humble people are those who know their strengths and weaknesses, are confident in who they are, and yet know that input from others can only make things better and protect them from a blind spot. Proverbs commends this approach. "Plans are established by taking advice; wage war by following wise guidance" (Prov. 20:18).

Albert Black, founder of On-Target Supplies & Logistics, knew he needed advice and the benefit of outside expertise when his company surpassed the 10-million-dollar mark (see the online video "Seek Out Advice," in "Proverbs and Work" at www.theologyofwork.com). So he sought the advice and insight of others, including John Castle, one of Dallas's leading executives and

Albert's board chairman and mentor. Albert wasn't afraid to ask for advice, nor did he think it made him look weak. He was thrilled to have someone with Mr. Castle's wisdom and experience counsel him, knowing it would only help him and his business. Shrewd people acknowledge their weaknesses and blind spots and seek advice from others around them.

The book of Proverbs constantly cries out, "Listen, receive, and pay attention to my instruction and wisdom!" (see 1:8; 4:1; 5:1; 7:1). We all need someone in our lives who can mentor and advise us as we walk the path of righteousness.

 Food for Thought

Are there people in your life who are willing to share their wisdom and experience? Do you seek their advice or listen to their counsel? If you don't have a trusted, godly mentor in your life right now, how might you go about finding one? Name an incident where good advice saved the day. Remember a situation that went poorly where you did not seek counsel or advice beforehand. What happened and what did you learn?

_____

_____

_____

_____

_____

_____

_____

_____

Wise Men and Women

While seeking counsel is necessary for success, it is incredibly important to choose the right people as counselors. Just because people are older and seemingly wiser doesn't mean they are able to give godly counsel. We must seek wise men and women who are full of wisdom and understanding that flows from a fear of the Lord. For "no wisdom, no understanding, no counsel, can avail against the LORD" (Prov. 21:30).

Have you ever sought counsel from someone and acted on it, only to realize later that they didn't share your motives or values? Your outcome was probably not good. Proverbs 13:20 says, "Whoever walks with the wise becomes wise, but the companion of fools suffers harm." It is all about the company we keep and whose counsel we seek. Remember, "Iron sharpens iron, and one person sharpens the wits of another" (27:17). Surrounding yourself with wise people who will challenge you is a godly directive for your good. Be discerning and discriminating when choosing your friends, associates, and mentors.

As a Christian, you have the Spirit of truth abiding in you, and he "will guide you into all the truth" (John 16:13) when you listen to his "still small voice" (1 Kgs. 19:12, KJV). "When you turn to the right or when you turn to the left, your ears shall hear a word behind you, saying, 'This is the way; walk in it'" (Isa. 30:21). The Holy Spirit, through the confirmation of our conscience (Rom. 9:1), will guide us in truth—of this you can be sure. And if we are equipped with the Holy Spirit and the counsel of wise advisors (Prov. 11:14), we are sure to keep our feet from evil and on the path of righteousness.

 *Food for Thought*

If "iron sharpens iron," who in your life sharpens you? Describe a situation where you received the counsel of the Holy Spirit and felt his leading. Are you surrounding yourself with wise people?

_____

_____

_____

_____

_____

_____

_____

_____

Closing Prayer

Thank God for those in your life who give wise counsel and sharpen you. If you are in need of a mentor and godly associates, pray about it. Give thanks for the Holy Spirit's guidance and all those who have given you sound counsel along your way.

Lesson #3: Lifelong Learner (Prov. 1:5; 18:15; 19:23; 31:17)

Keeping Pace

Have you ever worked with or known someone who refused to keep up with the times? Maybe they decided computers weren't for them or that their land telephone line was "good enough." Perhaps change was too difficult, and they wanted everything to stay just the way it was. When people refuse to learn, grow, adjust, and adapt to new things, new people, new ways, new technology, or new structures, they usually render themselves out of touch. Learning how to live and function in an ever-changing environment is a critical characteristic of the wise worker. It is those lacking shrewdness who refuse to adapt and who wind up losing their jobs, suffer demotion, quit, or become bitter.

In Proverbs 31:17, we see the Valiant Woman girding herself with strength and making her arms strong. She does what it takes to keep pace with the work before her. Teachers constantly have to take continuing education courses to keep up with new requirements and methods. The business world offers conferences and seminars that enhance and expand education beyond college and graduate school. Shrewd parents are always educating themselves on the next stage of development for their children, knowing that the skill set needed for teenagers will be different from the skill set used for preschoolers. If you want to remain as effective as possible in what you do, you must keep pace.

 Food for Thought

How have you kept pace with your changing environment and its demands? What are some of the changes you see coming in your industry or vocation that will require adaptation and preparation on your part? Is there anything you have refused to accept or accommodate to because of your preferences and comfort zone? If so, what do you think you need to do?

_____

_____

_____

_____

Drawing Near

If a shrewd person is a lifelong learner, it seems we would be missing the point if we thought our learning and development concerned only our work and not our relationship with God. He wants us to be lifelong learners of him. True wisdom for the Christian involves the whole revelation of God, especially as known in his Son, Jesus Christ. As we grow in our understanding of the Lord, we learn how to cooperate with him as he sustains and redeems the world. This often makes us more fruitful, in ways that benefit ourselves and in ways that help others. It causes us to revere the Lord in the midst of our daily life and work. Proverbs 19:23 says, "The fear of the LORD is life indeed; filled with it one rests secure and suffers no harm." There is no end to the spiritual life in Christ Jesus. James 4:8 says, "Draw near to God, and he will draw near to you." It's not complicated. As you work to keep abreast of changes and remain relevant in the workplace, do not forget your relationship with God—the source from whom all blessings flow—and press on to all God has for you each day. As you do, he will draw near to you.

 Food for Thought

Do you have a daily discipline that feeds your soul so that you grow in the wisdom of the Lord? How can you grow in your relationship to God?

Closing Prayer

Ask the Lord to stir you to continue growing in your work and in your relationship with him. Thank him for his friendship and leading. Thank him for all the opportunities he has afforded you to develop as a person and to draw closer to him.

Chapter 5

The Wise Worker Is Generous and Just

"There is an inequitable distribution of both goods and opportunities in this world. Therefore, if you have been assigned the goods of this world by God and you don't share them with others, it isn't just stinginess, it is injustice." —Timothy Keller, *Generous Justice: How God's Grace Makes Us Just*

Lesson #1: A Lifestyle of Generosity (Proverbs 3:3; 11:24–26; 19:17; 28:27; 31:19–20)

Counterintuitive

Somewhere inside each one of us is a fear whispering that if we live generous lives we will come up wanting down the road, but Proverbs teaches the exact opposite:

> Some give freely, yet grow all the richer; others withhold what is due, and only suffer want. A generous person will be enriched, and one who gives water will get water. The people curse those who hold back grain, but a blessing is on the head of those who sell it. (11:24–26)

> Whoever is kind to the poor lends to the LORD, and will be repaid in full. (19:17)

> Whoever gives to the poor will lack nothing, but one who turns a blind eye will get many a curse. (28:27)

Proverbs teaches that it is the one who gives to the poor who will be blessed and repaid in full, but people who withhold things from others will be cursed by a lack of things themselves. If we really believe the truth of this teaching, we will look for ways to be generous to those in need. If the Lord has blessed you with all you need, then he is also asking you to trust him while you give to those less fortunate.

 Food for Thought

How has God blessed you or put you in a position to be generous to those in need? If you're not financially secure yourself, should you still be generous to others? Have you ever experienced that it truly is "more blessed to give than to receive" (Acts 20:35)? Explain.

_____

_____

_____

_____

_____

_____

Her Hands

The hands we use to produce the things we need are the same hands we use to give generously to others (Prov. 31:19–20). In verse 19, the Valiant Woman puts her hands to the distaff (a staff that holds a wool or flax bundle) and holds the spindle as she spins her yarn or thread. In verse 20, she opens those very same hands to the poor, reaching out to the needy. Her work and her generosity are one motion. They are inseparable. Her hands flow back and forth between the actions of working and giving. It is important to note that the Valiant Woman is able to give to the poor and help the needy because of her hard work. Her diligence enables her to have something to give, and she gives it freely.

Proverbs 3:3 teaches that we are to walk in loyalty and faithfulness. Different biblical translations use the words *love* and *mercy* or *kindness*. Whatever the translation, we are instructed to never let the virtue of caring for others leave us. We are told to "bind them [loyalty and faithfulness] around your neck" and "write them on the tablet of your heart." The Valiant Woman is a beautiful example of someone whose hard work and generosity seamlessly flow from one hand to the other while she walks in mercy and kindness.

 Food for Thought

Do you have any practices in which you regularly give to those in need from the proceeds of your hard work? We are not supposed to have only generous moments, but we are called as Christians to live generously. What does that mean to you? Is there someone God is bringing to mind who would benefit from the gift of your time or your resources?

_____

_____

_____

_____

_____

_____

Closing Prayer

Thank the Lord for all he has blessed you with and whatever ability he has given you to work. Think about how God has been generous *toward you* and then give him thanks. Ask him how he wants you to be generous to others.

Lesson #2: It's a Matter of Justice (Proverbs 3:27–28; 14:21, 31; 16:8; 17:5; 21:13; 22:8–9, 16, 22–23; 28:8; 29:7; 31:20)

Proverbs does not stop with commending generosity but goes further to claim that caring for the poor is a matter of justice. First, we need to recognize that people are often poor because the rich and powerful defraud or oppress them. Or, if they were already poor, they have become easy targets for further fraud and oppression. This is abhorrent to God and he will bring judgment against those who do it. Second, even if you have not defrauded or oppressed the poor, God's justice requires that you do what you can to set things right for them, beginning with meeting their immediate needs.

> If you close your ear to the cry of the poor, you will cry out and not be heard. (21:13)

> Those who despise their neighbors are sinners, but happy are those who are kind to the poor. (14:21)

> Do not withhold good from those to whom it is due, when it is in your power to do it. Do not say to your neighbor, "Go, and come again, tomorrow I will give it." (3:27–28)

That helping the needy is a matter of justice, and not merely one of generosity, is no surprise if we remember that wisdom rests on the fear of the Lord. That is, wisdom consists of living in awe of our God so that we seek to do what he desires for the world. God is just. God desires that the poor be cared for and poverty be eliminated. If we truly love God, then we will care for those whom God loves. Therefore, to relieve the poor and to work to eliminate poverty are matters of justice.

Justice is not only a matter of sending a donation, but of working, and perhaps even living, alongside poor people. It may mean working to break down the segregation of the poor from the middle class and wealthy in housing, shopping, education, work, and politics. Do you come into contact with people of higher and lower socioeconomic status on a daily basis? If not, your world may be too narrow.

Before we can heed the call in Proverbs to be "kind to the needy" (14:31) and share our "bread with the poor" (22:8–9), we actually have to *see* them. It is easy for all of us to live cloistered lives—unaware and unmoved by what surrounds us—but God is calling us to do the opposite. This week, look around you as you go about your business. Whether you work in a big city or a small town, there are needs all around you. Make a conscious effort to see those you pass by on a daily basis.

 Food for Thought

Are you aware of the people who are in need in and around your place of work? Do you know what your co-workers' needs are? Their familys' needs? Those of your customers or the consumers of your work? Those of the people you pass by on your way to work? How could you become more aware of people's needs through your work?

_____

_____

_____

_____

Right a Wrong

The book of Proverbs treats caring for the poor as a matter not only of generosity but also of justice. Justice involves not only caring for those in need but righting a wrong. Justice gives people what they are due but cannot get on their own because of a wrong done, oppression, bad fortune, lack of opportunity, or illness. There are people who have dedicated their careers to a mission of justice. There are others who find ways to make generosity and justice flow out of their "ordinary" work, whatever it may be.

In his article "What Is Biblical Justice?" (*Relevant Magazine*, August 23, 2012), Timothy Keller explains that the word *justice* occurs more than two hundred times in the Old Testament and essentially means "giving people what they are due, whether punishment or protection or care."

We serve a just God. As wise workers, we are called to do justice, to care for those in our society who are most vulnerable. If justice is "giving people what they are due," we must ask what the widow is due, the child left alone and abandoned, the elderly. What about those who profit by exploiting children and trafficking in sex slavery? How are we as Christians to make wrong things right, to help the powerless, and protect the vulnerable, the migrant worker, the refugee, or the homeless?

As we draw closer to God, he changes us and we become more like him over time. What once seemed hard becomes easier as we live out our lives in relationship with Jesus. Our hearts start to overflow with his love, causing us to want to do justice, to love kindness, and to walk humbly (Mic. 6:8). It's a river of life flowing out of us.

Food for Thought

Who are the powerless, needy, oppressed, or vulnerable that you encounter in your work? In what practical ways could you help them? How can you work for justice not only in your workplace but throughout society?

_____

_____

_____

_____

_____

_____

_____

_____

Closing Prayer

Ask God to soften your heart and open your eyes to those near you who need your assistance. Ask God to show you "who," and then tell you "how" you should open your arms and extend your hand to the needy. Ask God to let you feel how he feels. Thank God for choosing you as an instrument of his justice.

Lesson #3: A Response Is Required (Prov. 8:15; 16:12–13; 22:9; 24:17; 25:5, 21–22; 29:4, 14)

Corporate Response

God cares for others and so should we. When you study the life of Jesus Christ, you see how he spent his time. During his ministry years, in between teaching, he stopped to feed the hungry, heal the sick, and defend the vulnerable. He fed five thousand people with loaves and fish (Matt. 14), healed the sick (Matt. 8), and protected the adulterous woman about to be stoned (John 8). Jesus didn't live a cloistered life, but interacted with the needy, oppressed, and defenseless. Christ and God's word teach us over and over again to take care of those around us.

The Valiant Woman continues to stand before us as our example. She "opens her arms to the poor and extends her hands to the needy" (Prov. 31:20). As a manager of a household containing multiple businesses and workers, she demonstrates a focus beyond the immediate and personal to the corporate or communal with an eye toward helping those around her. Many companies are excellent models and have an extraordinary history when it comes to caring for those in need and being generous. As wise workers, we not only need to challenge ourselves to help others but also challenge our workplaces to do the same.

 Food for Thought

Share examples of business, government, or other organizational strategies that attempt to defraud or oppress the poor and take advantage of the ignorant or vulnerable. Share examples of the opposite. Does your workplace have a history of helping those in need and protecting the vulnerable? If you or your place of work are not in the habit of helping those less fortunate, why do you think that is? How would you change it?

_____

_____

_____

_____

_____

_____

Radical Response

Radical as it may seem, Proverbs even instructs us to treat our enemies and competitors with generosity and justice. "If your enemies are hungry, give them bread to eat; and if they are thirsty, give them water to drink; for you will heap coals of fire on their heads, and the LORD will reward you" (Prov. 25:21–22). In Romans 12:21, the Apostle Paul challenges his readers by quoting this very proverb, adding, "Do not be overcome by evil, but overcome evil with good." We also read in Proverbs 24:17, "Do not rejoice when your enemies fall, and do not let your heart be glad when they stumble." What? Is God really calling us to be kind and generous to our enemies and our competitors?

Democracies and market economies rise in general due to the benefits of competition. Healthy competition actually fosters growth, productivity, and an environment where individuals and organizations thrive. We are to compete vigorously, but this does not mean seeking to destroy our competitors. Companies go out of business, but their successful rivals should not become monopolies. Elections have winners and losers, but the victors do not rewrite the constitution to ban the losing party. Careers rise and fall, but the proper penalty for failure is not "You'll never work in this town again," but "What help do you need to find something better suited to your talents?" Godly wisdom means learning how to engage in competition that makes the most of each player's participation and offers a soft landing for those who lose today's contest but who may make a valuable contribution tomorrow. Proverbs assures us that by treating competitors with kindness and justice, we are not putting ourselves at a disadvantage, but opening ourselves to be part of God's blessing of the world, even through competition.

 Food for Thought

How has the Lord rewarded you in the past when you engaged in competition or struggled with generosity and kindness? Practically speaking, how can you as a worker or an organization bless your rivals and extend kindness and generosity to your competitors? Would doing so strengthen or weaken your organization?

_____

_____

_____

_____

_____

_____

Closing Prayer

Thank God for all the individuals and corporations who have heeded God's call to help those less fortunate. Pray for their continued success and strength. Ask God to show you how you can live a more radical life by loving your enemies and blessing those you compete with.

Chapter 6

The Wise Worker Guards the Tongue

He who has knowledge spares his words,
and a man of understanding is of a calm spirit. (Prov. 17:27)

Lesson #1: The Negative and the Positive (Proverbs 6:17, 24; 10:20, 31; 12:18–19; 13:3; 15:2, 4; 16:1, 27–28; 17:4, 20–21; 18:20; 20:19; 21:6, 23; 25:15, 23; 26:20, 28; 28:23; 31:26)

A Perverse and Unguarded Tongue

Did you know there are more proverbs about the tongue than about any other topic? Proverbs 21:23 reminds us that to "watch over mouth and tongue is to keep out of trouble." God made everything to be used for good, especially the tongue. But since the fall of humanity, everything that is good can be used for evil. James 3:6 says, "The tongue is a fire. The tongue is placed among our members as a world of iniquity; it stains the whole body, sets on fire the cycle of nature, and is itself set on fire by hell." With that said, it seems pretty important to learn to guard and bridle our tongues!

Proverbs 18:21 says, "Death and life are in the power of the tongue." The proverbs tell us that a person by simply speaking can shed innocent blood (6:17), break the spirit (15:4), bring on calamity (17:20) and trouble (21:23), and encourage evil (17:4). The tongue is a mighty weapon and, unless we take care, we can cause immeasurable damage to the people and institutions that surround us.

Something as simple and seemingly innocuous as gossip can bring strife, discord, and damage to a person or organization. Proverbs says that the "words of a whisperer are like delicious morsels" (18:8), tasty when tripping off the tongue, but devastating to colleagues, friends, and neighbors (16:28–29). So when people gather around in the break room and start to gossip, get up and walk away. Or, better yet, change the conversation and save everyone some trouble. Proverbs 20:19 tells us that "a gossip reveals secrets; therefore do not associate with a babbler." Pretty plain and simple.

Communication is an important component of our lives in the workplace. The damage that an uncontrolled tongue can cause through gossip, angry outbursts, sarcasm, derogatory statements, cutting remarks, and inappropriate humor is vast. It's no wonder that Proverbs tells us, "An intelligent person remains silent" (11:12). James picks up this advice in the New Testament when he says, "Be quick to listen, slow to speak, slow to anger" (James 1:19).

 Food for Thought

Have you seen how a "perverse and unguarded tongue" can cause damage in your workplace? Can you give some examples? Why is the tongue so difficult to control? Is gossip a part of your work environment? Are you part of it? How could you respond? How can you better control your tongue and be one who is "slow to speak"?

_____

_____

_____

_____

_____

_____

_____

_____

A Righteous and Gentle Tongue

It's not all bad news when it comes to our mouths. A righteous and gentle tongue can bring wisdom (Prov. 10:31), healing (12:18), knowledge (15:2), life (15:4; 18:21), and the word of the Lord (16:1). It truly is amazing the good you can do with a righteous and gentle tongue.

Approach your workday wondering how you could use your tongue to bring blessing, wisdom, healing, knowledge, life, or the word of the Lord to someone. Blessing others at work could be a worthy goal resulting in a ripple effect of goodness. When is the last time you purposed yourself to control your tongue and use it solely for good, from your first morning coffee to the minute you headed for home?

 Food for Thought

Think of someone who has a righteous and gentle tongue. How has their communication affected you? How does controlling your tongue improve your life and work?

_____

_____

_____

_____

Closing Prayer

Ask the Lord through the power of his Spirit to help you control your tongue and use it for good. Pray that God heightens your awareness of how your tongue can be a positive or a negative force at work. Ask for his help and guidance in this area of communication.

Lesson #2: Kindness, Not Anger (Proverbs 11:17; 15:1, 18; 16:32; 19:11, 21; 31:26)

His Kindness

When we walk the path of righteousness with kindness, we are walking as Christ walked and loving as God loves. To bring that virtue into the workplace—extending mercy, kindness, and love to customers, competitors, clerks, lawyers, professors, CEOs, assistants, students, maids, cooks, and colleagues—would not only positively affect them, but us as well. God accomplishes much through our kindness.

In Proverbs 31:26, the Valiant Woman "opens her mouth with wisdom, and the teaching of kindness is on her tongue." It is the hope of all companies that their customers will be dealt with kindly. It's good business. The wisest organizations know that customer complaints can be viewed as opportunities. Even though anger is the natural response to an irate, screaming customer on the phone, good customer service organizations learn how to respond with compassion and kindness—winning over the customer and solving the problem at hand. All of us would do well to develop that habit. Proverbs 15:1 says, "A soft answer turns away wrath, but a harsh word stirs up anger." Usually responding in kind to an angry customer, co-worker, or supervisor causes only more trouble, but a soft response can have far-reaching positive results.

In Romans 2:4, Paul tells us that it is God's kindness that leads us to repentance. God doesn't use anger, guilt, manipulation, avoidance, or coercion. He uses kindness. We should do the same.

 Food for Thought

Is kindness prevalent in your workplace? Is it valued? Give examples. Why does kindness matter? How can you teach kindness (like that of the Valiant Woman) in your workplace?

_____

_____

_____

_____

_____

_____

_____

Managing Your Emotions

Human development theorist Arthur Chickering explains the process of identity development through the use of seven vectors or stages that deal with feeling, thinking, believing, and relating to others. The level of an individual's development in each of these vectors contributes to the strength of their ability to function with stability and intellectual complexity. The second of his spectrum of seven vectors is managing our emotions. This task consists of learning to understand, accept, and express emotions. If we cannot manage our emotions, our ability to function with stability and intellectual complexity is considered low.

Throughout Proverbs, the rewards of being able to manage our emotions are highlighted and this behavior is strongly encouraged.

> Those with good sense are slow to anger, and it is their glory to overlook an offense. (Prov. 19:11)

> Those who are hot-tempered stir up strife, but those who are slow to anger calm contention. (15:18)

> One who is slow to anger is better than the mighty, and one whose temper is controlled than one who captures a city. (16:32)

The beauty of these proverbs is that they also provide a picture of the person who can deal successfully with anger. The Bible, however, doesn't teach us *not* to be angry. Anger is sometimes the most appropriate response when dealing with sin. Ephesians 4:26 says, "Be angry but do not sin; do not let the sun go down on your anger." We are allowed to be angry, but we must know how to manage the emotion so we don't sin. By the power of the Holy Spirit dwelling in us, we can be slow to anger, respond with a soft answer, and be a calming influence in a contentious atmosphere.

 Food for Thought

What does responding in kindness, not anger, require of you? What are some of the positive results or fruits of such behavior? When have you seen emotions managed well in the workplace? When have you seen emotions not managed well in the workplace? What were the results?

_____

_____

_____

_____

Closing Prayer

Ask for the peace and kindness of God to fill your spirit as you walk the path of righteousness at work. Ask that his character be reflected in your actions. Thank God for his great kindness toward you and for being a God who is slow to anger and full of loving-kindness.

Lesson #3: Apples of Gold in Settings of Silver (Proverbs 10:31; 12:18, 25; 15:1–4, 18; 16:1; 18:21; 25:11–12, 25; 31:7–8)

The Power of Words

When you're in the company of people who are gossiping, complaining, and talking about ways to get even or get ahead, it certainly doesn't make you feel good. We've all been there. As negative as that scene is, we get lured in because there is something in our nature that likes to vent, make others look less than ourselves, and hear a "juicy story" about someone. It's enticing on a certain level. But when you run into someone with some good news, or your supervisor delivers a great review on your yearly performance, or you have a productive conversation with a colleague and solve a problem, or someone just encourages you with a good word that makes you smile, you feel the heaviness lift that you didn't even realize was there. Words are powerful.

God spoke the world into being through his words (Gen. 1), and Jesus is the Word that became flesh and lived among us (John 1:14). The psalmist tells us that by treasuring God's word in his heart, he was kept from sinning against God (Ps. 119:11). Proverbs teaches us that a righteous and gentle tongue brings wisdom, healing, knowledge, life, and the word of the Lord.

The Valiant Woman opens her mouth with wisdom, and the teaching of kindness is on her tongue. You can picture her with her workers using a soft answer to turn away wrath (see Prov. 15:1), and when she ran into a hot-tempered person stirring up strife, you can be pretty sure she was slow to anger and calmed the situation (Prov. 15:18). If we follow her example, consider the positive impact we would have on people and our environment.

 Food for Thought

Are you aware of the power of the spoken word? How have you seen the power of words used for good at your company? For bad? What can you do to be more thoughtful when using words in the workplace? Think about the many ways used to communicate today through personal conversation, texting, e-mails, social media, and so on. Today, more than ever, our words can have a far-reaching effect, so it is vital to use your words wisely.

_____

_____

_____

_____

_____

A Blessing or a Curse

As always, we have a choice to use our tongue to bless others or curse them. Proverbs 12:25 says, "Anxiety weighs down the human heart, but a good word cheers it up." Just like that you could alleviate someone's anxiety and give that person a reason to smile—all with the power of your words.

God calls us to live in a different way—a way more concerned about those around us than ourselves. It is radical but incredibly good. In Proverbs 25:25, good news is likened to "cold water to a weary soul." Weary, anxious, discouraged people surround us. The wise worker is someone who takes the time and opportunity to bless people and change their day. Who knows what would happen if we all kept our tongues from evil and used them thoughtfully throughout the day to bring blessing and encouragement?

 Food for Thought

Remember a time when someone spoke a good word to you or encouraged you. How did it affect you? Describe aspects of your workplace that are encouraging and aspects that are negative. How could you use your words to bless someone? How have e-mails, texts, and social media made the topic of "guarding your tongue" even more important? Take some time to encourage one another.

Closing Prayer

Ask the Lord to make you aware of how you speak. Pray for the self-control to bridle your tongue and to be slow to speak. Ask him to bring to mind someone who needs some encouragement or a good word, and pray about how and what you might do to build up that person. Ask the Lord to help you be a person who constantly and consistently uses words for good.

Chapter 7

The Wise Worker Is Modest

"God measures people by the small dimensions of humility and not by the bigness of their achievements or the size of their capabilities." —Billy Graham

Lesson #1: The Mother of the Vices—Pride (Proverbs 3:5–6; 6:16–19; 11:2; 16:5, 18–19; 21:4; 29:23, 25)

Are You Proud?

It's good to take pride in what you do. That kind of pride produces excellence, which the Lord values and calls us to (Prov. 31:26). When someone gives you a pat on the back for a job well done, whether literally or figuratively, you should feel good. Everyone needs affirmation, encouragement, and a clue that they are heading in the right direction. But that is not the pride being spoken of here. "Pride goes before destruction, and a haughty spirit before a fall. It is better to be of a lowly spirit among the poor than to divide the spoil with the proud" (Prov. 16:18–19).

What is it about pride that causes people to be destroyed, humiliated, and disgraced? Proverbs tells us that "when pride comes, then comes disgrace" (11:2), that pride "will bring humiliation" (29:23), and that "all those who are arrogant are an abomination to the Lord; be assured, they will not go unpunished" (16:5).

It's been said that "humility is the foundation of all virtue, but pride is the essence of all sin" (Harold Vaughan, "The Great Sin," April 2012). God not only hates pride, but he even hates a prideful look. In Proverbs 6:16–19, there are seven things listed that the Lord hates, and *first* on the list is "haughty eyes." Think about that.

As we have seen, Proverbs teaches us to live in a healthy fear of the Lord. We need to acknowledge who we are (the created ones) and who God is (the Creator). God longs to care for his children, and he knows that living humbly under his care is the best, safest, most enjoyable and successful way for us. If we are going to walk with God, humbling ourselves and bending our knee to his authority is the only way.

 Food for Thought

Can you cite any workplace examples where pride caused a fall from grace, humiliation, or destruction? In what ways would pride deter a healthy, good relationship with God? How is pride the essence of all sin?

_____

_____

_____

_____

_____

_____

The Right Perspective

God wants us to be diligent workers, adding quality and value to what we do and produce. He wants our work to matter and make a difference in the lives of others. More than anything, God wants to walk with us—even at work—and transform our character to become ever more like his own.

Walking in humility and modesty helps us keep the right perspective and relationship with God. Oftentimes, when we achieve a level of success where our needs are more than met and we are on the receiving end of a lot of praise and attention, our minds wander. When things start going well, we tend to get off our knees and drift away from God. We start believing our success is because of us—our hard work, talent, and cleverness. This is where pride enters in and we get separated from the One who loves us—the source from whom all blessings flow.

Proverbs 29:23 says, "A person's pride will bring humiliation, but one who is lowly in spirit will obtain honor." Not only will walking in humility keep you from disgrace and destruction, but it will actually bring you honor. Again, God's ways can seem counterintuitive, but they are always true and better.

 Food for Thought

Name someone who has walked in modesty and humility, resulting in honor. What can be done to maintain the right perspective and a posture of humility? How did Jesus set an example for us to follow?

_____

_____

_____

_____

_____

_____

_____

Closing Prayer

Ask the Lord to keep your heart humble as you continue to stand in awe of who he is. Ask him to reveal to you areas of pride you might currently be unaware of in your life. Thank God for the example of his Son, Jesus Christ.

Lesson #2: What Drives You? (Proverbs 11:28; 13:8; 18:11; 22:1; 23:4–5; 28:22; 30:7–9)

False Security

The ancient sage Agur—the source of the next-to-last collection of sayings in the book of Proverbs—records his heartfelt prayer in which he asked God to give him "neither poverty nor riches" (Prov. 30:8), seeing that *either one* could draw him away from God. We work to earn a living, enjoy a measure of comfort and security, and to provide for others. Many of us work because we feel called to our vocations by God's leading. But if we turn our work into a quest for ever-increasing wealth—in other words, if we are greedy—we have left the path of wisdom. To help us avoid that tendency, Scripture teaches us to pursue God above all else, not money.

Again, God's instruction is for our good. We can all think of people who are obsessed with wealth, and we have seen the consequences of a life so lived, confirming the proverb, "Better is a little with the fear of the LORD than great treasure and trouble with it" (15:16). Wealth lures us with its false promise of security, yet the Bible teaches that our security and trust should be in the Lord. "Do not wear yourself out to get rich; be wise enough to desist. When your eyes light upon it, it is gone; for suddenly it takes wings to itself, flying like an eagle toward heaven" (23:4–5). Proverbs 18:11 speaks to the false sense of security wealth can bring: "The wealth of the rich is their strong city; in their imagination it is like a high wall."

In 1 Timothy 6:17, the Apostle Paul sums it up well: "As for those who in the present age are rich, command them not to be haughty, or to set their hopes on the uncertainty of riches, but rather on God who richly provides us with everything for our enjoyment."

 Food for Thought

It is hard not to be lured by wealth. Our culture—perhaps every culture—values the wealthy, and wealth offers its fair share of temptations. What would it look like—practically speaking—not to put your trust in riches?

_____

_____

_____

_____

_____

_____

_____

The Lie

At some point in our lives we have all probably said something like, "If I could just make a bit more money, I would be set." The problem with that is we always seem to need even more once we arrive at the place we thought would be enough. We may seek wealth—consciously or not—because it seems to offer concrete evidence of our success and self-worth. Our insatiable appetites for comfort and security are never quite satisfied—unless we put our faith in God.

God knows how the lure of wealth can adversely affect a person, which is why he calls us to be driven by him and his wisdom, not money. The warnings are clear. Wealth is "a ransom for a person's life" (Prov. 13:8). "Those who trust in their riches will wither" (11:28). "Loss is sure to come" to the miser who is in a hurry to get rich (28:22). But we are encouraged with the truth that "whoever trusts in the LORD will be enriched" (28:25).

Wisdom cries out to us to trust in God and not believe the lie that wealth will bring life and security. We would do well to heed her call and remember the proverb, "Happy are those who trust in the LORD" (16:20).

 Food for Thought

What is most striking to you about this lesson? What is your "take-away"? How can wealth hold you captive? How can we work diligently and provide for those around us without being driven by the lure of wealth?

_____

_____

_____

_____

_____

_____

_____

Closing Prayer

Pray for each other, that the Lord will "satisfy every need of yours according to his riches in glory in Christ Jesus" (Phil. 4:19). Ask the Lord to keep you from the temptation of wealth and ask that he alone would be what drives you in your work.

Lesson #3: Conclusion—All Good Things (Proverbs 10:22; 14:24; 15:6; 22:2; 30:10–11, 16, 18, 20–22, 31)

A Blessing from the Lord

The book of Proverbs is not opposed to wealth itself. Obviously, wealth can be a great blessing and source of good. "The blessing of the LORD makes rich, and he adds no sorrow with it" (10:22). It is the obsession with wealth that gets in the way of our relationship with God and diverts us from the path of righteousness. In 1 Timothy 6:10, Paul reminds us that it is the *love of money* that is the root of evil, not money itself.

Wise workers who are modest possess an attitude of thankfulness as they work diligently, knowing that every good thing is a result of grace from a loving God. The Valiant Woman runs a successful household and "she is more precious than jewels." Proverbs 31 extols her for her earnings and purchases (v. 16), her profitable merchandise (v. 18), her ability to clothe her household in crimson, purple, and fine linen (vv. 21–22), and the deservedness of the "fruit of her hands" (v. 31). It is the blessing of God that makes someone wealthy—whether or not they recognize the source from whom all good things flow. "The rich and the poor have this in common: the LORD is the maker of them all" (22:2).

 *Food for Thought*

If God has blessed you and your organization with wealth, it is important to ask how you are going to use his blessing to bless others. When we see that God is the source of our wealth and ability to provide, what should our response be?

_____

_____

_____

_____

_____

_____

_____

_____

Conclusion—God's Good Plans

God is intensely concerned with and interested, involved, and invested in our work and in all we do. "For human ways are under the eyes of the LORD, and he examines all their paths" (Prov. 5:21). He is rooting for us and wants us to succeed in a way that pleases him.

Wisdom is God's guide for those who have chosen to follow God on the path of righteousness. By giving us his wisdom, he orders "all our steps" (20:24), makes our labor profitable (14:22), keeps the righteous from harm (12:21), shows us favor (12:2), gives us treasure (15:6), lets us prosper (28:25), and establishes our plans (16:3). As Jeremiah 29:11 puts it, "For surely I know the plans I have for you, says the LORD, plans for your welfare and not for harm, to give you a future with hope." All the instruction, teaching, admonition, and promises in the book of Proverbs are there for our good, to lead us on the path of righteousness. God's own wisdom gives us the ability to trust God to shape our destiny and take charge of our ends. "Commit your work to the LORD, and your plans will be established" (Prov. 16:3).

 Food for Thought

Consider all that the Lord has given you and how he has blessed your work as you have followed him, then share with each other God's goodness in your life.

_____

_____

_____

_____

_____

_____

_____

Closing Prayer

Thank the Lord for the good plans he has for your life and work and ask him to give you the wisdom to walk in his ways. Ask him to make you aware of his presence in your work every day and of the ways he protects and blesses you there.

Wisdom for Using This Study in the Workplace

Community within the workplace is a good thing and a Christian community within the workplace is even better. Sensitivity is needed, however, when we get together in the workplace (even a Christian workplace) to enjoy fellowship time together, learn what the Bible has to say about our work, and encourage one another in Jesus' name. When you meet at your place of employment, here are some guidelines to keep in mind:

- *Be sensitive to your surroundings.* Know your company policy about having such a group on company property. Make sure not to give the impression that this is a secret or exclusive group.

- *Be sensitive to time constraints.* Don't go over your allotted time. Don't be late to work! Make sure you are a good witness to the others (especially non-Christians) in your workplace by being fully committed to your work during working hours and doing all your work with excellence.

- *Be sensitive to the shy or silent members of your group.* Encourage everyone in the group and give them a chance to talk.

- *Be sensitive to the others by being prepared.* Read the Bible study material and Scripture passages and think about your answers to the questions ahead of time.

These Bible studies are based on the *Theology of Work Bible Commentary*. Besides reading the commentary, please visit the Theology of Work website (www.theologyofwork.org) for videos, interviews, and other material on the Bible and your work.

Leader's Guide

Living Word. It is always exciting to start a new group and study. The possibilities of growth and relationship are limitless when we engage with one another and with God's word. Always remember that God's word is "living and active, sharper than any two-edged sword" (Heb. 4:12). When you study his word, it should change you.

A Way Has Been Made. Please know that you and each person joining your study have been prayed for by people you will probably never meet but who share your faith. And remember that it is "the LORD who goes before you. He will be with you; he will not fail you or forsake you. Do not fear or be dismayed" (Deut. 31:8). As a leader, you need to know that truth. Remind yourself of it throughout this study.

Pray. It is always a good idea to pray for your study and those involved weeks before you even begin. It is recommended that you pray for yourself as leader, your group members, and the time you are about to spend together. It's no small thing you are about to start and the more you prepare in the Spirit, the better. Apart from Jesus, we can do nothing. Remain in him and you will "bear much fruit" (John 15:5). It's also a good idea to have trusted friends pray and intercede for you and your group as you work through the study.

Spiritual Battle. Like it or not, the Bible teaches that we are in the middle of a spiritual battle. The enemy would like nothing more than for this study to be ineffective. It would be part of his scheme to have group members not show up or engage in any discussion. His victory would be that your group passes time together going through the motions of just another Bible study. You, as a leader, are a threat to the enemy as it is your desire to lead people down the path of righteousness (as taught in Proverbs). Read Ephesians 6:10–20 and put your armor on.

Scripture. Prepare before your study by reading the selected Scripture verses ahead of time.

Chapters. Each chapter contains three lessons. As you work through the lessons, keep in mind the particular chapter theme in connection with the lessons. These lessons are designed so that you can go through them in thirty minutes each.

Lessons. Each lesson has teaching points with their own discussion questions. This format should keep the participants engaged with the text and one another.

Food for Thought. The questions at the end of the teaching points are there to create discussion and deepen the connection between each person and the content being addressed. You know the people in your group and should feel free to come up with your own questions or adapt the ones provided to best meet the needs of your group. Again, this would require some preparation beforehand.

Opening and Closing Prayers. Sometimes prayer prompts are given before and usually after each lesson. These are just suggestions. You know your group and the needs present, so please feel free to pray accordingly.

Bible Commentary. The Theology of Work series contains a variety of books to help you apply the Scriptures and Christian faith to your work. This Bible study is based on the *Theology of Work Bible Commentary*, which examines what the Bible says about work. This commentary is intended to assist those with theological training or interest to conduct in-depth research into passages or books of Scripture.

Video Clips. The Theology of Work website (www.theologyof-work.com) provides good video footage of people from the marketplace highlighting teaching on work from every book of the Bible. It would be great to incorporate some of these videos into your teaching time.

Enjoy Your Study! Remember that God's word does not return void—ever. It produces fruit and succeeds in whatever way God has intended it to succeed.

> "So shall my word be that goes out from my mouth;
>   it shall not return to me empty,
> but it shall accomplish that which I purpose,
>   and shall succeed in the thing for which I sent it." (Isa. 55:11)

Explore what the Bible has to say about work, book by book.

GENESIS 1-11

LUKE

PROVERBS

PHILIPPIANS

JAMES

THE BIBLE AND YOUR WORK
Study Series

THEOLOGY OF WORK · PROJECT